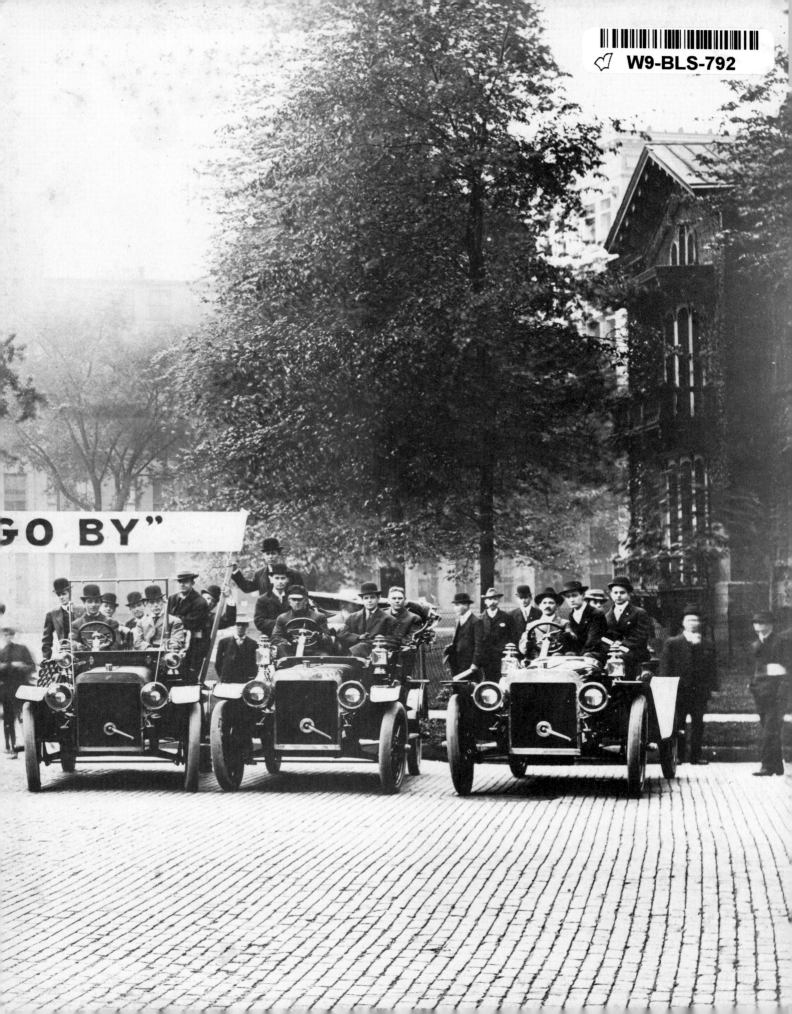

Endpaper

Enthusiastic new Model K Ford owners rally at Detroit in 1906 with Henry Ford and a soon-to-be-famous advertising slogan. The auto genius may be seen among the derbies, leaning to his right, below the word ''Go.''

Fords Forever

Fords Forever

BY LORIN SORENSEN

Old Fords never die, they just keep on going! A well-worn but faithful Model T (left) delivers the mail in York County, Maine, in 1930.

A Silverado Publishing Company Book

Acknowledgements

A very special thanks to Roy Jones for the authentic color illustrations produced for this book. And to Ford Parts and Service Division for selecting them for the 1983 Motorcraft Calendar art. Also to Diane Hamilton for her photo research in Washington, D.C., and to Bill Honda, Dean Batchelor, Bob McCoppin, Greg Sharp, LeRoi Smith, Marty Jones, and Neal East for their inspiration.

Production Credits

Lithography preparation, Dave Ruiz; Copy Production, Gail S. Mulkey; Copy Editor, Valerie Presten; Production Assistant, Edy Sorensen; Cover and inside color illustrations, Roy Jones; Typesetting by Digi-type; Graphic Services by Herdell Printing. Printed and bound by Kingsport Press, Kingsport, Tennessee.

Library of Congress Cat. Card Number: 82-80166
ISBN 0-942636-01-5

They went together like Mom and apple pie—a pretty girl and a 1931 Model A Ford Roadster.

Ford was the undisputed king of the early dirt tracks. A starter at the 1934 Gilmore Gold Cup at Los Angeles brings a row of fired-up Ford V8 roadsters to the line.

Contents

Like one of the family, the Ford has been a familiar figure around the yard for most of this century. The rustic owners of this 1938 Ford Deluxe Tudor were small truck farmers, shown peddling fall squash from their front yard along the Mohawk Trail in Massachusetts in October, 1941.

Just an ordinary farm family buying a new 1939 Ford Standard Sedan—but the beginning of a true romance.

Foreword

Pictured opposite is just an ordinary farm family buying a new Ford V8. And, yet, this simple scene probably comes as close as any in this book to capturing the real essence of the Ford mystique.

The captivating photo was found by our researcher Diane Hamilton in an unlikely National Archives file marked "Federal Crop Insurance." On the back was penciled, "Lincoln, Nebraska." There was no date but the comely sedan is obviously a 1939 model, and the informal gent to the right looks as though he might be the salesman.

That part of the U.S. is corn country and my guess is that the farmer has put on his Sunday best to take his well-scrubbed family in to town to shop with some of the insurance money covering a weather-damaged or failed crop. A FCI bureau photographer has likely tagged along to get some documentary shots for Roosevelt's "New Deal."

We know what the father is thinking about. He's considering price and terms, gas mileage . . . and, maybe, whether the car has enough road clearance to get them through the winter snows and spring mud. Little sister is tired and would just like to curl up in the big mohair back seat and go to sleep.

Now, look at Mom. She is a pleasant lady who looks much older than her years because farm life is lonely and hard on a woman. But you can see the wheels turning in her head about all the things she can do with this car—like attending church socials more often, and taking little trips to town with her egg money.

The bright-faced kid in bib overalls already knows his dad is going to buy the Ford and has positioned himself to be the first one to climb in. It is a day he will never forget and in later years could recall to the nickel what the family got in trade on the old Model A for the shiny blue V8; the ride home by Cousin Wilbur's to show it off; and what a good car it was through the years.

Only another memory, but part of the colorful kaleidoscope that has made the Ford automobile such an important part of American life.

Lorin Sorensen
St. Helena, California

1

That Old Ford Magic

The golden era spanned forty years.

It began in late 1908 when Henry Ford captivated neophyte buyers with the first of his smashingly successful Model T's and ended the year following the auto maker's 1947 death, with the last of his still-irresistable V8's. In that dynamic time other swell cars would come down the pike but none would touch more American lives, or spawn greater legends than the Ford.

Henry's cars had a special magic from the start. The tough, compact, featherlight Model T matched the average man's pocketbook and had become so popular by the end of 1913 that, while the cars were streaming from the Detroit factory at the rate of one every three minutes, there was a waiting list of 100,000 buyers. As one competitor complained, "the durn Fords aren't sold, they're just handed over the counter."

At the peak of popularity in 1925 the Model T's were being produced at the rate of a new car every ten seconds and accounted for half the auto production in the U.S. But, in the decade that gave birth to jazz, bathtub gin, and buying on margin, price had lost its charm. Suddenly the Model T was doomed in the shift to cars with more color and style.

Model A replaced Model T for 1928 in the most sensational new car introduction of all time. It seemed the entire nation was standing in line for one of the trim beauties and even chic Hollywood got in on the act. Douglas Fairbanks bought his wife Mary Pickford a Sport Coupe for Christmas. Will Rogers, Cecil B. De Mille, and Louis B. Mayer bought Tudors, and Billie Dove, Wallace Beery, Lon Chaney, and Lillian Gish took delivery of other models.

The stylish Model A rode in on a bull market and it looked like Henry Ford had another long term winner—good for fifteen years or more—like the Model T. But it wasn't to be. After setting a blistering sales pace, the car crashed with the stock market and the aftermath of stiffer competition called for another major change.

Ford outflanked his competitors and their smooth "sixes" by bringing out an all-new body style with an unprecedented low-price V8 engine in 1932. For a man near 70, it was a stunning achievement—dulled only by the sluggish economy of the Great Depression. The V8 years were, in many ways, his most imaginative. Certainly, an admiring public would look forward to his yearly styling changes and come to know by heart the many subtleties of his evolving V8 chassis and body designs.

In all, Henry Ford would give the world nearly 32 million wheeled vehicles in his lifetime. On the following pages we'll take a photographic ramble around the U.S. in the earlier days to rediscover what made those cars of his so extra special.

Henry Ford (1863-1947), genius of motors, never lost touch with life's simple pleasures. Shown in a relaxed moment, he holds some children spellbound with his pocket watch.

The hills and vales and winding streams,
    The meadow lark's glad song
Are calling, ever calling me
    To leave the surging throng.
I grasp the wheel of my Model T—
    A sturdy little car—
And through the city's crowded streets
    Speed on to fields afar.
                    Walter McComas, 1914

Henry Ford's Model T caught on like wildfire. Here, a proud owner poses with his new 1909 Roadster.

Two fashionable ladies go places in their 1912 Model T Torpedo Runabout that they wouldn't have before.

New York City, New York, 1909

Put simply, the reason the Model T was such a stunning success was that people loved it. The 4-cylinder car adapted to any road; it held up rain or shine; and best of all it cost under a thousand dollars. The derbied gentleman at the left, pictured on a Sunday drive in New York's Central Park, was so infatuated with his dandy Ford that he branded it with his own initials in bold brass script.

Boise, Idaho, March, 1912

Ford Motor Company was just five years old in 1908 when it struck gold with the Model T. By 1912 they were everywhere and even the less adventurous ladies were giving up their dappled mares and sprite buggies to learn the crank and throttle levers—and the system of floor pedals that made the thing work. With the new freedom, two Oregon ladies are pictured above visiting in neighboring Idaho. A relative has put the pet Labrador on the car's hood for a picture.

Grandpa gets the seat of honor in a 1915 Ford Touring. Advent of the Model T brought new leisure to Americans.

Tacoma, Washington, September, 1921

If a man worked hard and saved every penny, his reward might be a brand new Ford. The plucky dock worker at the right stuck to his goal until he could buy the best Model T in the showroom—a 5-passenger, 4-cylinder, 20 horsepower Sedan. He is pictured on a brief detour to work, picking up his new car at Blangy Motor Company in Tacoma. The dealer and his sales staff—looking a bit smug—have loaded the car with such extras as two-tone disc wheels, speedometer, and two-tone body paint, to bring the tab to about nine hundred dollars.

A begrimed Tacoma laborer with his first car—a 1921 Model T "centerdoor" Sedan

A fellow with a Ford was considered a pillar of success. Four proud owners of new Model T coupes pose for a dealer

promotional photo at Tacoma, Washington, in 1923.

Some friends prepare for a spin about town in the driver's new 1923 Model T Touring car.

It was a bit tight but the 1923 Model T Coupe could seat three adult passengers across.

Illustration by Roy Jones

One of five Model T passenger car body types offered in 1923 was the quite fashionable Fordor Sedan.

Detroit, Michigan, 1923

The main reason people could afford to buy Henry Ford's automobiles was because he always stuck to his home-spun belief that "the only thing that makes anything not sell is because the price is too high." The proof of that principle reached its greatest glory in 1923 when the price of the basic Touring car was dropped to $295 and the Model T set all sales records. That was also the year the stately 5-passenger Fordor Sedan became available—giving many families their first chance to enjoy the spacious comforts of a fully-enclosed car. Above, and opposite, some Ford buyers sport about the motor city in their suddenly-affordable, and very jaunty, new Model T's.

Seven available Model T body styles displayed at a large Louisville showroom in 1926

A 1926 Model T Touring in the foreground of a Ford display at the Doss-Jones agency in Louisville

To help increase the city's size, Louisville sent this 1927 Model T Touring on a sales junket.

Louisville, Kentucky, April, 1927

In one of the last hurrah's for the incomparable Model T Ford, Louisville city boosters sent one on a razzle-dazzle tour of 34 middle-America cities to drum up some real estate business. The flashy touring car was fresh off the local assembly line and had been given a special white paint job and red wire wheels and lettering. Three volunteers wearing white flannel knickers, red and white checked sweaters and golf socks, and white shop coats took turns at the wheel and are shown at city hall eager to set off on the publicity caper.

One of the first Model A Fords seen in Washington, D.C., was this handsomely-styled 1928 Sport Coupe.

Washington, D.C., December 2, 1927

It was the evening of the most sensational new car introduction of all time. There had not been a new Ford built since the last of the out-of-date Model T's came off the line six months earlier and interest in its replacement had become a national curiosity. At the Company's Washington showroom, the branch manager and his smartly-dressed wife have their picture taken with one of Henry Ford's wildly anticipated Model A's (a Tudor Sedan) just before the doors were swung open to let in an eager crowd. Displayed at one end of the showroom (above) is an alluring Sport Coupe— the first Ford with an optional rumble seat and forerunner of a complete line of imaginative Model A body styles.

"The Model A introduction was probably the best advertising on a new model we ever had. It was so great that on our first showing people were willing to pay to get in to see this new car. When we showed it in Chicago we caught one of the janitors charging a dollar to let people in the back door, the crowd was so jammed."

Fred L. Black,
Ford advertising manager

Tacoma, Washington, 1929

Henry Ford kept thirty assembly plants across the nation working day and night building Model A's—and still the demand was astonishing. The Tacoma dealers were supplied by Seattle and offered this all-Ford show in late 1929 to ballyhoo the latest body styles. On the floor with their rumble seats open are a Roadster (near left) and a Sport Coupe. A Cabriolet with its top collapsed sits just beyond the pert roadster.

Tacoma dealers were swinging on the stars, with all of the Model A Ford sales written up at this show staged in 1929.

Ladies visiting at Louisville, Kentucky, with their sporty 1929 Model A Fordor Sedan

A 1930 Model A Town Sedan,

A Ford salesman

Dearborn, Michigan, May 12, 1931

It took nearly 20 years to sell 15 million Model T's, but less than four to deliver 5 million of the colorful assortment of Model A's. Even so, Ford dealers had their work cut out if they wanted to make a sale to some of the old die-hard ''flivver'' owners. At the right a hawk-eyed salesman shows a prospect that the gravity-flow gas tank built into the cowl won't explode in the driver's lap, and that the pedal on the right is the foot brake. The simple gas tank design had caused an uproar with insurance companies (the tank would be found harmless) and Model T drivers had to learn to cope with the A's shift lever and clutch instead of the 3-pedal transmission floor controls which had been in use for two decades.

Roadster, and two-window Fordor Sedan on sale at a Louisville, Kentucky, Ford agency

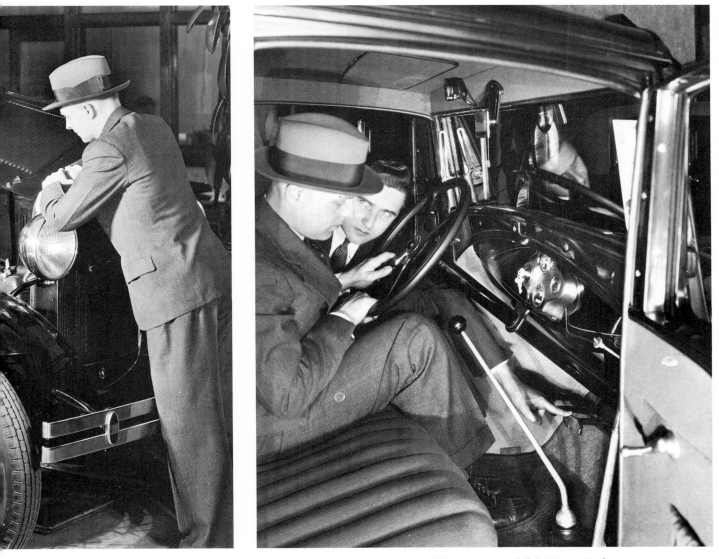

acquaints a customer with some of the important mechanical features of the 1931 Model A Town Sedan.

A camera in the balcony captures the moment at the 1931 Tacoma Auto Show Ford exhibit.

Screen starlet Gladys Ford with a sporty 1931 Model A Deluxe Roadster

Burbank, California, 1931

Last of the splendid Model A's, the 1931 Fords were high-fashion motoring for any crowd. Movie tough-guy Edward G. Robinson had one (above) brought to the studio between breaks in filming *Little Caesar*. While he was thinking over the purchase from dealer Henry Perrin, the quick-witted Warner publicity photographer used it as a prop to model the young movie hopeful pictured above.

Tacoma, Washington, 1931

At an all-make auto show (left) held in the civic auditorium, some Tacoma-area Ford dealers pose for the camera while the evening crowd mobs the exhibits. Model A's on the show floor include two sedans, an exciting new Victoria, and a Coupe, while on stage a fashion show is just ending.

Dealer, Henry Perrin, delivering a new 1931 Model A Convertible Sedan at Los Angeles, California

Flowers for Madame, with door service by a high-class 1931 Model A Ford Town Car Delivery

A 1931 Model A Town Car Delivery on a street in New York state

Illustration by Roy Jones

Hollywood, California, 1931

Shops of distinction needed a delivery car of refinement so, in 1931, Ford offered this ritzy model, shown at an estate. It featured a handsome all-aluminum body in a wide choice of fashionable colors, a veneer-panelled parcel space, exquisite side lamps, and an open chauffeur's compartment.

Curious Texans examine Henry Ford's new V8 engine—under the hood of a 1932 Ford Standard Coupe.

Showrooms were loaded with Ford V8's in mid-1932, but wary customers were scarce. This dealer got some action

Brady, Texas, April, 1932

Fresh from the assembly plant in Dallas, a 1932 Ford (facing page) attracts a crowd of locals eager to see the much-publicized new V8 engine up close. That the cars were the most beautifully designed Fords yet seemed trivial to all the commotion over the change from a reliable ''four'' to a chancy ''eight.''

A pretty secretary models a 1932 Ford Standard Coupe at Brady, Texas.

with a P.T. Barnum-type test drive promotion.

Long Beach, California, August, 1932

When the controversial new V8's first appeared in April, 1932, it wasn't easy for Ford dealers to convince old 4-cylinder customers of the car's better utility—especially in the deepening Depression. So, to get people behind the wheel of one of these dandys, Melone Ford staged a carnival-style open air show of new models near Long Beach and offered free drives over a bouncy ''test course.'' Shown in front of his agency is H.O. Melone and drivers with the ''Phantom Fleet'' test cars—four Fords stripped to the bare essentials to demonstrate the marvel of V8 engineering.

Sweethearts speed along a pleasant country road in their nifty new 1932 Ford V8 Deluxe Roadster.   Illustration by Roy Jones

Ann Arbor, Michigan, July, 1932

Surely the ultimate motoring adventure for a young sport in 1932 was to be breezing along in a fast new Ford roadster with the windshield folded, the top laid back, and a pretty girl by his side. Of all the Fords built before or since, none have had as much classic appeal as this legendary rag top.

Bound for the country club in her well-dressed 1933 Ford 5-window Deluxe Coupe

Palm Beach, Florida, 1933

The 1933 Ford models were all new and rakishly handsome, but the pretty owner of this one wanted a few extra details, in keeping with her sporty set. Daddy had special-ordered his darling daughter's car with an all-white paint scheme (regular 1933 models had black fenders), elaborate pin striping, and white wall tires. The dealer added on some fancy accessories such as wind wings, bumper guards, and a running greyhound radiator cap.

The Elegant Lincolns

Master of the low-priced car market, Henry Ford didn't overlook the chance to provide an automobile for the aristocrats as well. When the Leland family was forced to put its Lincoln Motor Company on the block in 1922, he bought the prestigious firm lock, stock, and hubcap, and put his refined son, Edsel, in charge. The result was some of the most beautiful automobiles ever produced in America—and the cornerstone of Ford's quality image to this day. During most of the Edsel era, Lincoln coachwork was further complimented by the custom creations of such body companies as Judkins, Brunn, Willoughby, Murray, and Dietrich. Engines were always either V8 or V12.

Tending a big 1936 Lincoln V-12 sedan

Edsel Ford's graceful Lincolns were classics in their own time. A gentleman poses with his new 5-passenger Coupe on the golf links at Louisville, Kentucky, in 1933.

A Louisville society matron with her 1929 Lincoln Dietrich Convertible Coupe

Famed race car builder Harry Miller with his new 1931 Lincoln LeBaron Convertible Roadster at Lincoln head-quarters in Detroit

Star of this airy showroom is a 1934 Ford Deluxe Tudor with sporty white wall tires.

Tacoma, Washington, June, 1934

Brilliantly styled, from the sweep of the heart-shaped grille to the well-turned back bumper, the 1934 Fords were low-priced classics. Featured at National Motors alongside a Fordor, 5-window Coupe, and a Victoria, is a pretty Tudor Sedan with Tacoma Cream wheels and pin stripe. Little doubt the origin of the stylist who named that popular shade of Ford paint.

Waring band members at the Detroit train station in a glamorous 1934 Ford Phaeton

Film actress Mona Barrie, poised at the beach with her racy 1934 Ford Cabriolet

Lake Arrowhead, California, August, 1934

Relaxing at Arrowhead Lodge after making her film debut in *Carolina*, starlet Mona Barrie is called upon to pose for some Columbia Studios publicity stills. Her gorgeous soft top V8 was specially fitted by dealer Henry Perrin in Los Angeles, and features Vogue white wall tires and 16-inch Kelsey-Hayes wheels.

Detroit, Michigan, August 10, 1934

Famed band leader Fred Waring and his Pennsylvanians toured their radio show nation-wide in 1934—sponsored by the Ford Dealers of America. One of the eye-catching Ford V8's sent out by Edsel Ford to meet the maestro in the motor city was this posh Phaeton (left) carrying the girl singing trio and frog-voiced drummer Poley McClintock.

Mother is thrilled when father brings home a new 1935 Ford sedan.

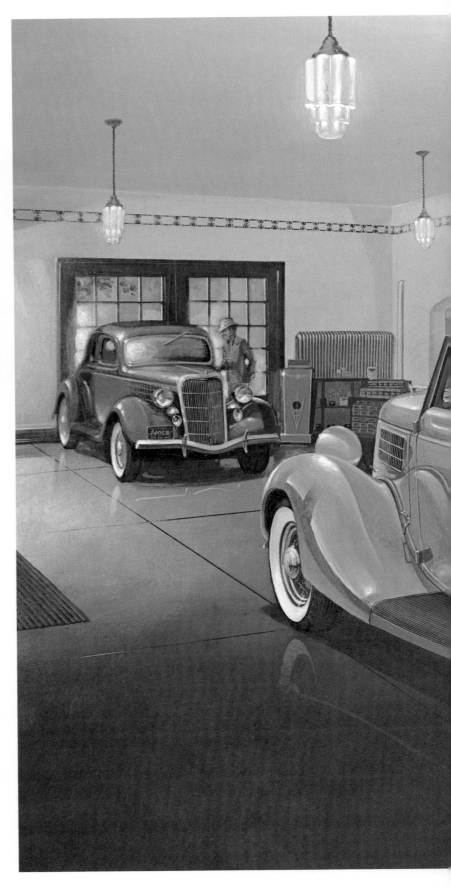

Louisville, Kentucky, 1935

Buying a new car has always been an exciting experience. Here, a mother and daughter swoon over a stunning Cabriolet finished in Cordoba Gray (tan), with Poppy Red wheels and pin stripe. Dad is impressed, but is mindful of the $625 price tag. Extra passengers could be carried in the rumble seat of this model, which tipped back by turning the deck handle. Riders got in by first stepping onto the rear bumper and then onto a rubber step pad mounted on the right fender.

Illustration by Roy Jones

42

A young family visits a Ford dealer's showroom and falls for a breath-taking 1935 Cabriolet.

The first Fords with optional fender skirts were the 1937 models. A Deluxe Fordor Sedan takes a Los Angeles family to church in style.

A handsome family enjoys a sunny outing in a distinctive 1936 Ford Convertible Sedan.

Juvenile star Jackie Cooper and Rin-Tin-Tin Jr., with a brand new 1936 Ford Cabriolet.

Philadelphia, Pennsylvania, 1937

There seemed no end to the variety of Fords produced during the 1930's. At the left, a suburban family beams happily from one of the more unusual open models to appear in 1936. This was the trunk-style Convertible Sedan, which meant that it had a clam-shell deck lid built into the rear body for luggage stowage—compared to the earlier model which had a flat rear body. The all-weather collapsible top was ideal for the active family.

Hollywood, California, 1936

On a back lot in tinsel town, the wonder dog and boy hero of the golden screen pose with their driver between takes of the 1936 movie, *Tough Guy*. The showy jet black V8 was bought by Warner Brothers Studios for the duo's use around town.

Window shoppers in Tacoma study the gleaming V8 exhibit chassis at Mallon Ford.

Elongated by the camera, a 1938 Ford Deluxe 5-window Coupe sits waiting for a buyer.

Hydraulic brakes for the first time, and pleasing body lines were well received on the 1939 Fords.

Louisville dealers get a preview of the new 1939 Ford, Lincoln-Zephyr, and Mercury cars.

Tacoma, Washington, November 22, 1937

The thing dreams are made of. When Tacoma's Mallon Ford put the new 1938 Fords and Lincoln-Zephyrs on display, a big attraction was the 85hp show chassis (facing page, top) loaned by the branch sales office. Rubbernecks were continually awed at Henry Ford's genius in creating such a wonder of working parts.

Louisville, Kentucky, November, 1938

Recovered from the big Ohio River flood of 1937, which inundated it, the Louisville Ford assembly plant was back to "business as usual" when its sales office put on this show for area dealers and their families. The crowd is pictured looking over the new 1939 Ford and Lincoln lines —as well as the just-introduced Mercury car.

Lincoln-Zephyr, Mercury and Continental

In a bid for a share of the middle-income market, Henry and Edsel Ford brought out a quick succession of imaginative new car lines toward the end of the 1930's. The ultra-streamlined 1936 Lincoln-Zephyr made its debut as the industry's first mass-produced unibody automobile, and was followed in late 1938 by the new Mercury—a longer, roomier, more stylish version of the regular Ford V8. Continental was the daring European-influenced entry for 1940, and a car Edsel Ford accurately predicted would attract the luxury sport car buyer. In the end, while highly regarded for their noble ride and sleek lines, the V12-powered Lincoln-Zephyrs were far ahead of the market and faded out in 1942. Mercury and Continental carried on to be among Ford's great successes.

The M.E. Hannon's, of Anacortes, Washington, taking delivery of the 100,000th Mercury, at Dearborn, Michigan, January 18, 1940

A futuristic 1937 Lincoln-Zephyr Sedan—one of the Ford-built streamliners too advanced for the times

An archery outing with a sporty 1941 Continental Cabriolet. Winner of numerous design awards, these early V12 Continentals were in a class by themselves and were available in either the coupe or convertible body styles.

An otherwise drab Detroit intersection is brightened by a flashy 1940 Ford Deluxe Tudor Sedan.

Detroit, Michigan, September, 1942

At Cadillac Square in the motor city, a trio of Fords led by a well kept 1940 model, stop at a pedestrian crosswalk. The attack on Pearl Harbor was still a fresh memory and the War Board's order to ration gasoline and tires, and to drive only when necessary, seemed well heeded. Notice that the busses nearly equal the cars in this scene—all of them urging drivers to "Ride Our Tires."

Visiting at Stockton, California, in 1940 with a new Deluxe Fordor Sedan

A demure agency model poses with the Deluxe variation of the Ford Tudor Sedan offered for 1939.

A newly-married couple wash their precious 1941 Ford Sedan during World War II.

Stepping out for the evening in Dearborn, Michigan, with a modish 1941 Ford Super Deluxe Fordor

Childersburg, Alabama, May, 1942

It was wartime and anyone with a fairly new car was lucky, because it would have to last for the duration. At the left, ammunition plant worker Albert Smith and his wife Fay, demonstrate for government publicity how they planned to preserve their Ford ''by constant care and slow driving.''

Newest Ford on the block—a shapely 1942 Super Deluxe Sedan Coupe

Dearborn, Michigan, 1942

The long selling season of the modernistic 1941 Ford models came and went and folks had just gotten used to the idea of no running boards on the new 1942's when World War II broke out. Within weeks, Ford promotional picture-taking like that above and left would cease as Henry Ford turned his company's attention to military output.

Back making civilian cars after WWII, Ford stayed in the limelight with such activities as lending this fleet of fresh

A maple-bodied 1946 Ford Sportsman Convertible—new to the line—on display at a Detroit department store

1946 convertibles to hype a movie premiere.

Detroit, Michigan, 1946

Ford Motor Company rolled out five shiny new Ford convertibles when comedian Phil Silvers and the cast of *If I'm Lucky* attended the film's screen preview in Detroit. The fashionable cars are pictured with their drivers in front of the Fox Theatre, waiting to take the stars on parade. Ford was the first U.S. automaker to resume civilian car production after the WWII hiatus in which no 1943-45 models were made. Much admired of the post-War cars were the all-new Ford and Mercury Sportsman convertibles with their wood bodies—but they failed to find a market and were discontinued before the 1949 line came out. A similar fate was in store for the Continental, which did not reappear in the Ford car lineup until 1956.

Singer Mary Martin at the Dallas State Fair with a 1948 Continental Coupe—the last of this nameplate until 1956

2
A Few Laughs, A Few Distractions

Life with the Ford has had its lighter moments—and even the mishaps were sometimes good for a chuckle or two. Imagine the footage those rascally comics Laurel and Hardy, or W.C. Fields, might have immortalized from this incident as reported in the June 10, 1935, edition of the *St. Helena Star* (California) newspaper:

". . . Remo Corbella had a narrow escape Thursday evening of last week when, as he was cranking his Model A Ford, it started. Fortunately it was in reverse gear and went backward instead of forward. The car plunged across Oak Avenue, went between two trees, crashed through a fence and into the back of a house at the corner of Oak and Spring. As the car started backing, Corbella ran after it and fell, ruining his new trousers."

It was sure the stuff jokes were made of, since some of the flaws in the Ford character were downright legendary.

Trusty as it was, the Model T was infamous for picking the deepest mud or steepest grade to stop dead in its tracks with an occasional bout of burned-out bands or connecting rods. The Model A was just as easily a real kill-joy when the pesky water pump was leaking and the radiator was boiling over; and there was never a longer string of traffic that a whimsical flathead V8 wouldn't tie-up by coughing to a halt with terminal vapor lock.

But those were the bad days. As we will see on the following pages, Ford along the road was a many-sided adventure—from humor and breakdowns, to the ordinary pleasures of getting gas at a country store; visiting a garage or wrecking yard; watching an expert mechanic at his trade; riding a car ferry; or going camping.

You couldn't have the good times of Ford motoring without a little adversity. A New Yorker touring out west in his Model T is given some inspiration by his sweetheart, in taking up the burned-out connecting rods.

Two tenderfeet with their stuck 1918 Model T Touring car

Idaho, 1924

In the days when some roads wandered off through the sagebrush to a river bank and picked up again on the other side, fording shallow streams was commonplace. The Model T, with its high ground clearance and rugged constitution, usually took to the water with ease. But, in this case, the old "flivver" has hit a soft spot and its two riders are up to their shanks trying to extricate it.

A 1912 Model T Touring, hardly damaged from being on-end in a ditch

Helpful farmers use a tripod and block-and-tackle to haul out the sturdy Ford.

Racine, Wisconsin, 1912

The gleaming Ford was only a month old when it swerved to miss a stray cow and plunged off the road into a ditch. Aside from the driver landing head-first in some cockleburs, the only damage done was to his pride and to the sturdy car's top and windshield assembly. Nearby farmers summoned to hoist the Model T out of its embarassing position were astonished that, once righted, it would drive away with nary a wobble.

Double steering wheels in a 1924 Model T Coupe

Leonard car with controls for two

Tacoma, Washington, 1924

Since a lot of people didn't know how to drive, it was the car salesman's job to teach them the tricks. The Leonard Ford agency in Tacoma hit on the idea of giving greenhorn customers a spin around town in a dual-controlled Model T before seeing them off in their shiny new purchase.

The twin Mueller boys of Louisville in 1926 with their coming-or-going Siamese Model T

A comic driver with a shortened-up Model T stunt car

Louisville, Kentucky, September, 1925

Typical of the silly cars dreamed up for 4th of July parades is this Louisville Ford dealer's mascot car with touring Australian comedian Stub Pollard at the wheel. The wacky car mesmerized spectators with antics that ranged from running driverless in tight circles around its clowning driver, to responding obediently to his whistle commands. Manipulation of concealed levers was the secret.

A trick Model T Ford driver makes a timed exit from his flipped flivver at the Los Angeles County Fair in 1929.

Pezel's wild mechanical horse

Cincinnati, Ohio, 1924

Alfred Pezel is shown at the wheel of the Model T "Iron Bronco" he built to condition football players during training. The idea was to get them in the saddle and give them a ride to sharpen their reflexes. Wrote Alfred on his patent application, "The bucking 'hoss' rears, plunges, snorts and kicks and nobody can ride it to a successful termination."

Los Angeles, California, 1929

Model T cowboys did everything under the sun with the willing old tin Lizzie—from playing polo to roping steers. Carl Brady and a partner built circle roll bars on their stripped Fords and with a little stunt practice, took them on tour. The big crowd thriller (left) was the faked head-on, where Carl, instead, jack-knifed his Ford at the last moment and let her double-roll into a collision. He always "miraculously" emerged from the dust unscathed.

Laurel and Hardy's Favorite Mascot

Hollywood's funniest comedy team, Stan Laurel and Oliver Hardy, used the willing Model T Ford to great effect in some of their most hilarious two-reelers. In *Two Tars*, they were a pair of sailors with dates headed for the beach in a rented roadster. Stuck in a traffic jam, they jostle another car and trigger a classic destruction derby. In their 1930 film, *Hog Wild*, Hardy's nagging wife pesters him to install a radio aerial on their modest bungalow—but his clumsiness makes her nervous. To prove who's boss, he ignores her and calls on his side-kick Laurel for help. The two proceed to bring the family Ford into the act and succeed in not only wrecking the house, but the car also.

In their unforgettable comedy, Hog Wild, *Laurel and the Hardy's get their Model T sandwiched between street cars.*

The boys enlist Ollie's Model T to help put up his wife's radio antenna in Hog Wild.

A lady deftly changes a tire on her 1917 Model T Touring.

New Jersey, 1919

Making the rounds in her dusty Ford, a county home demonstration agent is detained by the roadside with a flat tire. Women brave enough to venture out alone on the early roads were just as able as men to make some repairs. Note the clapboard home and outhouse on the farm in the background.

Speeders beware! A Washington State motorcycle cop nabs a '28 Model A Roadster on a wet road near Olympia in 1929.

Five college boys cut-up with their Model T on a summer camping trip to the Michigan woods in 1925.

Like a scene from "Tobacco Road," a 1929 Model A Tudor gets a tire fixed.

Douglas, Georgia, July, 1938

A field hand patches an inner tube as his young sharecropper boss looks on. According to government photographer Dorothea Lange, who took the picture, "Fords are beginning to appear as a means of transportation for sharecroppers. They can take tobacco to town and bring supplies back, and also, to take workers to Florida for seasonal fruit picking jobs."

Swapping used ignition coils to fix a sick 1926 Model T Coupe

Abbeville, Louisiana, November, 1938

If the Model T had a common flaw, it was the spasmodic set of ignition coils that took their charge off the engine's flywheel magneto. Common practice among owners was to first swap coils with other derelict ''T's'' lying around, then try the local wrecking yard, and finally replace them with stock from the local Ford dealer. Here a farmer turns his problem over to the experienced hands of a cigar-chomping wrecking yard owner, who gives a suspect coil his practiced eye.

Pie Town, New Mexico, June, 1940

The farmer and garage man below work intently on the ignition of a battered Model A that once saw service as a taxicab. A broken windshield meant gnats in the teeth but a clean view for the driver. The community of Pie Town was settled in the early 30's by about 200 migrant Texas and Oklahoma farmers who filed homestead claims. The young garage man (hatless) came out from Texas to open a fairly thriving combined filling station, blacksmith shop and garage.

Fixing a flat on a '29 Model A Tudor in Michigan in 1940

Dogged determination will cure this 1929 Model A Town Sedan's ailments.

Cooling off a 1929 Model A Ford at Henrietta, Oklahoma, in July, 1939

A 1929 Model A Open Cab Pickup with borrowed wheels

Gassing up the 1931 Model A Tudor on the way to work

Atlanta, Georgia, March, 1936

A sharp garage man picked up extra cash by selling cast-off auto parts that accumulated. Here, secondhand tires, oddball hubcaps, inner tubes, wheels and fenders add interest to the false front of a shop in Atlanta. Judging from the assortment of wheels on the Ford "roadster" Pickup standing outside, its owner may have been one of the wall's best customers.

Atlanta, Georgia, June, 1939

Among fond memories of the Model A was the novel place it was fueled. Farmworkers watch a filling station attendant top off their car's tank located in the cowl below the windshield. Notice the car's gussied up front with its bug screen, headlamp shades and radiator ornament.

Watching the Fords go by from the front porch of a country store

Gordonton, North Carolina, July, 1939

In one of the all-time classic rural store scenes a proprietor and some of his customers lounge out front on a rustic porch. Off to the side a lone gas pump holds a few gallons in its glass, ready for the occasional car to stop by. Piled up stones support the rude building, and some limbed tree trunks make sturdy porch posts. Folks were made welcome by the wide plank steps and the signs advertising some popular brand goods.

Waiting for the cops to arrive at a wreck between a 1932 Ford Victoria and a 1931 Model A Fordor

A fancy 1930 Model A Roadster that rear-ended a bigger car at Louisville, Kentucky, October 10, 1936

Washington, D.C., September, 1932

What a pity! Odds would have it that a brand new Ford V8 would get singled out by a speeding Model A taxicab for a head-on collision at a capitol city intersection. Windshields bumped ajar by banged noggins saved serious injury.

Hollywood, California, 1932

W.C. Fields drove Lincolns but delighted in wrecking Fords in his movies. In *If I Had a Million*, his new 1932 Phaeton gets broadsided (right) by a "road hog." Given a million dollars by an eccentric who picked his name out of the phone book, Fields and his wife hire a gang to rid the city of road hogs. Their job done, they buy a new 1932 Ford sedan, only to be hit broadside by a milk truck as they are leaving the showroom.

Ford fans cringe when they see what W.C. Fields and Alison Skipworth do to a brand new 1932 Ford Phaeton in If I Had A Million.

Looking across the grassy parking lot of the Iowa State Fair in 1939

Des Moines, Iowa, September, 1939

Two dudes hoof it toward the midway past a sea of cars in this view of a typical 1939 fair in full swing. The abundance of Fords and Chevys attests to the farm country's conservative ways. In the left foreground sits a plain 1936 Ford Tudor.

Louisville, Kentucky, August, 1936

"Who'll bid $300 on this fine Ford?" Auctioneers (right) work their timeless profession at a hard-up Ford dealer's used car liquidation sale. On the block is a three-year-old Ford V8 Tudor sedan with snappy headlight visors. Other cars await their turn. Three bored little girls seem more interested in the photographer than in their fathers' try for a bargain.

One man's discarded tire could be another's stroke of luck, so this garage operator kept plenty on hand.

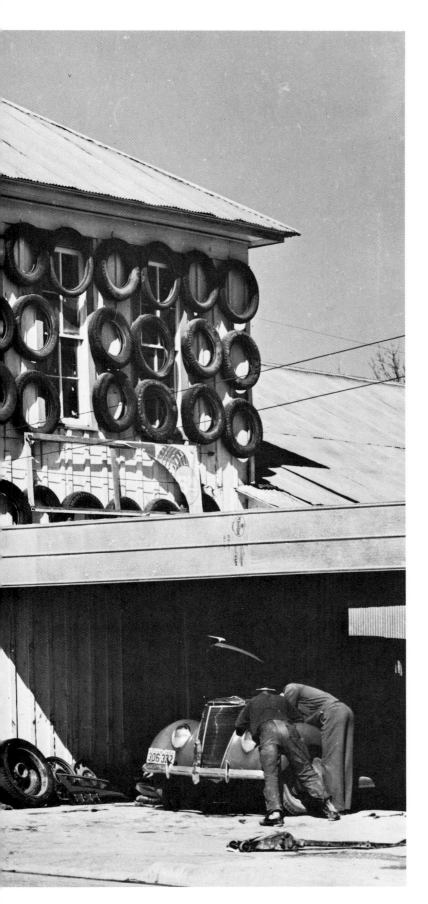

"... the garages with blazoned signs—
Used Cars, Good Used Cars. Cheap transportation, '27 Ford, clean. Checked cars,
guaranteed cars. Come in and look . . .

. . . Horsehair curling out of seat
cushions, fenders battered and hammered
back. Bumpers torn loose and hanging.
Fancy Ford roadster with little colored lights
on fender guide, at radiator cap, and three
behind. Mud aprons, and a big die on the
gearshift lever. Pretty girl on tire cover,
painted in color and named Cora . . ."*
John Steinbeck, The Grapes of Wrath, 1939

San Marcos, Texas, March, 1940

Used tires of all makes and sizes produce an artistic effect against the tall clapboard sides of this
busy shop. There was something here for every
car and pocketbook—baldies and regrooves,
knobbies and recaps, new, almost-new and
almost-shot tires of every description. A long
pole was used to retrieve selections, which were
hung high enough to thwart robbers when the
place was closed. Two mechanics work on a 1937
Ford sedan, as a 1929 Model A Ford coupe stands
at the island to get gas.

Steady hands and a set jaw win out over a 1934 Ford Coupe's stubborn piston.

Fort Bragg, North Carolina, June, 1939

When the old Ford started drinking oil, giving off clouds of smoke, and losing zip, it was time to think about giving it a ring job. The operation required dropping the engine pan and pulling the cylinder heads, then removing the rod bearings to free the pistons. This backyard mechanic shows the grit and intensity required to compress the new rings delicately onto the piston before its reinsertion back into the cylinder holes. One "shade tree" remedy for holding the individual rings in place when a ring compressor tool was not available was to wrap them with a piece of fine brass wire. The wire wore off when the engine started and actually built up a helpful brass glaze on the worn cylinder wall.

Arlington, Virginia, May, 1942

Using the rumble seat floor as a work platform, a veteran craftsman tacks down a new canvas top on a Ford roadster. The auto upholstery business boomed full tilt during World War II as the absence of new cars forced Americans to fix up their old ones. Convertible tops like this one cost about $35 installed in 1942. It is worthy to note that the 1937 model shown was the last of the sporty side-curtained Ford roadsters.

A 1937 Ford Roadster gets a new top.

Standing on a 1935 Fordor Sedan to get a better view

Yuma, Arizona, March, 1942

Paying little heed to the car's finish, some young farm workers watch a local rodeo on their day off. Letting his friends walk all over it this day, the owner has shown some previous affection for the car by modernizing it with a set of disc wheel covers over the ordinary wire spokes.

A stop for lunch with a 1936 Fordor Touring Sedan along a quiet New Hampshire road in 1942.

Waiting in a 1935 Fordor Touring Sedan for church to begin.

Greshamville, Georgia, June, 1941

Dressed in their Sunday best and waiting for the congregation to arrive, a young couple sit outside church in their Ford, listening to the gospel on the car radio.

It was June, 1940, and on the road outside Iowa Falls, Iowa, a 1938 Ford sedan skidded off into a corn patch. An investigating officer watches as some passing motorists pitch in to help a 1933 Ford tow truck winch it out.

Breaking down a flat tire on a 1940 Ford Deluxe Tudor Sedan

Washington, D.C., May, 1942

Clever service station mechanics learned early how to fix a customer's flat tire—without removing the wheel. This man is a classic study as he expertly works the bead off the rim so the tube can be removed. Once patched, the tube was reinserted and inflated and the car's owner would drive away thoroughly impressed.

Fixing a flat spare tire on a 1935 Ford Cabriolet in Washington, D.C., in 1942

"... Piles of rusty ruins against the fence, grease-black wrecks, blocks lying on the ground and a pig weed growing up through the cylinders ... In the grassy lot the wrecks lay, cars with twisted, stove-in noses, wounded cars lying on their sides with the wheels gone. Engines rusting on the ground and against the shed. A great pile of junk; fenders and truck sides, wheels and axles; over the whole lot a spirit of decay, of mold and rust; twisted iron, half-gutted engines, a mass of derelicts."

John Steinbeck, The Grapes of Wrath, 1939

Clarksburg, West Virginia, January, 1942

Like a passage from the John Steinbeck novel, a grave-yard for broken automobiles sprawls along a highway in the hill country of West Virginia. Fords were hard to kill and stayed on the road to the last gasp, but a few may be seen scattered among the relics.

Crossing a river by ferry in a scarcely-seen 1942 Ford Convertible

McCreary County, Kentucky, June, 1943

By chance, a camera captures one of the rarest Ford models as it rides the free cable ferry connecting Highway 90 across the Cumberland River. These 1942 soft tops were unusual because production was abruptly suspended after a short run, at the outbreak of WWII. On the road again, the driver could expect similar crossings over the many rivers that ran through this part of the country.

San Bernardino Co., California, July, 1938

Morning breaks over Grout Bay Camp (left) in San Bernardino National Forest, as the tent village comes alive. A scattering of Fords may be seen among the autos that have brought city folks to the mountains on vacation.

3

The Hard Times

Like the real-life scene on the facing page, and with Steinbeck's fictional Joad family in *The Grapes of Wrath*, thousands of displaced Americans would take to the road during the Great Depression.

Some abandoned their homes from total despair, while many were forced to flee the choking, billowing dust storms that blanketed much of Oklahoma, Texas, Kansas, Colorado and New Mexico. Entire towns were uprooted as people streamed toward the clear horizon in the west by thumb, truck or car—most often an old Ford. Sometimes there would be three generations of a family in a lone caravan of these jalopies rattling along Route 66 for the promised land with mattresses piled high and the wheezing, steaming cars straining hard for every mile.

The lure had been rumors of jobs aplenty and the fantasy that California was a paradise where folks lived "in a little white house beside an orange grove." For a stake in that dream they had traded in their skinny mules and broken plows for a worn out automobile, in hope that the old relic would take them far from their misery.

The Ford was a godsend in these painful times. It was plentiful on the used car lots at a cheap price; it was easy to fix and good on gas; and it was tougher than nails. In the end it would hold a very special place in the hearts of many who lived this tragic 1935-40 chapter of American history, and survived to find a new life.

Left among the legacies of that era is the impressive Farm Security Administration pictorial record on file in the Library of Congress. This was an immense government project where, by a stroke of luck, Roy Stryker was chosen to head a unit of photographers to document that the FSA programs were working and needed.

Stryker, a professor from Columbia University, saw it more than a propaganda job, but as an opportunity to capture the spirit of America on film. He hired out-of-work great, or soon-to-be great, artistic photographers such as Walker Evans, Russell Lee, Dorothea Lange, Marion Post Wolcott, and Carl Mydans, who, from 1935 to 1943, took one of the most extraordinary collections of photos of all time.

Among the nearly 200,000 prints on file are far more than the pictured loan benefits to farmers, and the new farm labor camps, but the faces of America on the streets and in the homes and churches across the land. Not overlooked was the back side of life with its crippling poverty, and migrants on the road with their old Buicks, Chevys, Dodges, Whippets, and the like.

What follows in this chapter is a heart-stirring selection of photos from the FSA files depicting travel by Ford.

". . . Listen to the motor. Listen to the wheels. Listen with your ears and with your hands on the steering wheel; listen with the palm of your hand on the gear-shift lever; listen with your feet on the floor boards. Listen to the pounding old jalopy with all your senses; for a change of tone, a variation of rhythm may mean—a week here? . . ."

John Steinbeck,
The Grapes of Wrath, 1939

Roofs piled high, odds and ends roped on, migrant cars were a familiar sight during the Depression. Here, a family of farm laborers rattle along in their faithful old Model A Ford in 1937 looking for work in California's hot central valley.

1924 Model T pointed west

Missoula, Montana, July, 1936

At the left, and facing page, young South Dakotans driven off their farm by drought rest on the way to rumored work in the Washington hop fields. They made about 200 miles a day in the Model T and slept nights in a tent.

Ukiah, California, February, 1936

Parlor up front and a bedroom in the back. The migrant couple below nailed together one of the earliest mobile homes, utilizing an old Ford chassis and bits of scrap. Comforts included a tilt-up roof, expandable bed, and window shades. Photographed at a pea picker's camp, the gent is telling the government photographer (Dorothea Lange), ''Ma'm, I've picked peas from Calipatria to Ukiah. This life is simplicity boiled down!''

This c. 1921 Model T camper could be on the road in a jiffy.

Roswell, New Mexico, May, 1937

It was a humbling experience for this farm family to ride a mattress out to California in search of work. They had first tried their luck in the Arizona cotton fields but were moving on for better pickings. Their forlorn Model T had once been a sporty black roadster before the homemade box was nailed on. Sideboards along the fenders mark the group as already roadwise—ready to make camp or pack up and leave at a moment's notice.

Bound for California, in a classic study of migrants

Once-proud Texans with their once-shiny 1923 Model T Roadster

Illustration by Roy Jones   *A young family stalled by the roadside with their 1929 Model A Fordor Sedan*

Odessa, Texas, May, 1937

They may be out of gas and stranded, but they haven't lost all hope. The father had worked in the oil fields but that played out suddenly and he was forced to pack up the wife and kids and strike out for California. Now he worries about selling his trailer to raise some cash. Note the Ford V8 wheels that have been swapped onto the front of his Model A from an earlier trade.

c. 1925 Model T loaded up with the bare essentials

Coachella Valley, California, February, 1937

Important goods wired slapdash onto the fenders and hood, a farm laborer's Ford prepares to leave a harvested carrot field for the open highway. Even the tire worn bald to the cord might come in handy somewhere ahead, and the baby's highchair and trunk can't be left behind. The owner put a covered platform (pictured right) on the back of the old coupe and bolted on some front fender braces to help haul his gear.

Fresno, California, November, 1936

The late afternoon sun catches a Model T loaded with bedrolls heading down US Highway 99. This time of year found field work scarce in California's central valleys, and many "fruit tramps" drifted south for the winter crops near the Mexican border.

1926 Model T Coupe on the road

A Texas migrant and the c. 1925 Model T Coupe he made into a truck

Sizing up the trouble with a backwoods Model T, c. 1922

Hamilton County, Tennessee, August, 1937

Household goods loaded willy-nilly on his stripped-down Ford truck, a displaced tenant farmer peers under the hood for the cause of his stall. Packed sand front tires were okay on hillbilly dirt roads, but out on the highway it looks like more misfortune ahead!

Flat tires were a regular part of this Ford's harsh existence.

Tulare, California, November, 1936

The old Ford's tires sang noisily along the hot pavement. Then, with a muffled bang, the left front casing let go and the driver brought the swaying pickup to a stop along the road's lonely shoulder. Flat tires were a common ailment among migrants wandering the highways in search of work. Here, a family from McAlester, Oklahoma, is delayed along a treeless stretch of macadam in California. Quite often the precious spare had been traded off for food or gas, in which instance the flat might be fixed with a "boot" inserted between the patched tube and the gash.

Fixing a flat on a 1929 Model A Pickup

Bakersfield, Calif., May, 1937

Migrant children observe the view from the back of the family Ford at a stop along US Highway 99.

Traveling handily in a 1926 Model T Open Pickup

Faded dreams and a once-pretty 1929 Model A Sport Coupe

Wandering Texans beside their busted c. 1920 Model T Truck

Shafter, California, November, 1938

Victims of a cotton pickers' strike, an apprehensive mother and daughter sit outside a Farm Securities Administration office while the father applies for an emergency food grant. Their car was bought in better times, and now they stand to lose it in trade for money to live on.

Lordsburg, New Mexico, May, 1937

Down on their luck, but not yet beaten, a family of drought refugees ponders the situation. They had traded off their tools for gas at the last town and now the old Ford had blown a head gasket. Loose rods could be taken up with bacon rind, and a piece of leather was good for a gasket; but without tools, they were stuck! Passing migrants were usually generous in lending a hand, but it was not uncommon for cars to camp along the highway for days while parts were hitchhiked for and repairs made.

1929 Model A Roadster in camp

Yakima Valley, Washington, July, 1936

A pitched tent in the woods is the temporary home for this man who just arrived from California to thin apples. The faithful Ford which brought him here will now take him to and from the orchards. Note the car's add-on radiator badge, headlamp shades, and the sideboards for carrying extra gear.

A 1928 Model A Business Coupe makes a good place to sit.

Kern County, California, September, 1939

Waiting for a job picking potatoes, a migrant Okla-
homan from Chickasha whiles away the time in camp.
His seat is the rear bumper of a Model A that has had its
wheels swapped for later ones. As the drought persisted
in the Midwest during the Depression, busted ex-farmers
like this man quickly supplanted Mexican labor in
California.

Loaded 1934 Ford sedan on the road to camp

Imperial Valley, California, 1939

Refugees from Wyoming arrive at a grower's camp for pea pickers. Desperate farm workers would take any pay, and newcomers to the fields were regarded with suspicion lest they underbid the force at hand.

The family Model T, taking a young boy to new places

Fort Gibson, Oklahoma, June, 1939

He never knew where the road might lead, but he sure knew where he had been! At the left a migrant boy peers pensively from his place at the back of a canopy-topped Model T pickup as the family tours Oklahoma looking for work. Roll-down side curtains and tidy belongings suggest a certain pride.

A farm labor contractor with his 1934 Ford bus at Santa Maria, Texas, in February, 1939

A battered 1928 Model A Phaeton has been faithful transportation for this family of eight.

"... The rag town lay close to water; and the houses were tents, and weed-thatched enclosures, paper houses, a great junk pile. The man drove his family in and became a citizen of Hooverville—always they were called Hooverville. The man put up his tent as near to water as he could get; or if he had no tent, he went to the city dump and brought back cartons and built a house of corrugated paper ..."

John Steinbeck,
The Grapes of Wrath, 1939

Vian, Oklahoma, June, 1939

The tragedy of her situation shows in the face of this mother as she worries how the family will scrape together the next meal. Barely 35 and aged before her time, the woman and her worn-out husband worked when they could as day laborers in the fields along the Arkansas River bottom. Six handsome children and an old Ford are all their possessions in the world. The car has lost its collapsible top and the upholstery is shot but it will be their only hope for moving on to a better life.

Camped in town beside a 1935 Fordor Sedan

Unloading a 1929 Model A Fordor in a government camp

Tulelake, California, September, 1939

Promised jobs in the potato harvest, a band of wandering farm workers set up camp across the road from the packing sheds. The four-year-old Ford made a dandy windbreak and anchor for the tarp covering the lean-to. Its seat cushions were jerked out at night for beds.

Merrill, Oregon, October, 1939

The broad flat roof of a Model A sedan was ideal for carrying a double mattress, and this gent has stacked it even higher. He had just arrived with his family for the Klamath Basin potato harvest and was assigned a tent in a labor camp set up by the Farm Security Administration.

Migrant kids hang around a tired-out 1931 Model A Tudor.

West Stayton, Oregon, August, 1939

At a shack town for bean pickers, some boys lallygag over a busted-up Ford. It was a Tom Sawyer life for many of these youngsters, who met new friends and picked up different tricks like chewing road tar and making sling shots. Through it all was the twang of ''Okie'' and ''Arkie'' accents blended with the drawls of Texas, Missouri, or Kentucky. Better-off kids could be told from the poorer ones because their patches were stitched on with a sewing machine.

Living out of a 1927 Model T Coupe

Prague, Oklahoma, June, 1939

Her husband is an out-of-work guitar player, and they can't even scrape together enough money to leave Oklahoma. The pain in this young woman's face speaks for the misery of sleeping in the car and cooking on the running boards. The badly abused Ford is still good for a lot of miles if they can only get some gas.

A 1930 Model A Tudor took these men to where the work was.

Homestead, Florida, 1939

Glad to have a job, four young migrant men from Tennessee lounge in the sun around their Ford while waiting for the shift change at a fruit packing shed. The car's spare tire cover proudly advertises their hometown.

4
Champion of the Working Man

There weren't too many things you couldn't get one of Henry Ford's lovable old Model T's to do.

If a gang of gandy dancers didn't have one up speeding along the train tracks, or a farmer didn't have one out in the field pulling stumps or raking hay, some clever fellow behind the next house would have one with the rear wheel jacked up sawing wood, or running the washing machine. Everything was tried at least twice on the trusty old "flivver" and when its tired bones were pushed over the bank to hold back the river, it was still picked over at low water for axle shafts to stake out the goat, and hood sides to patch the hen house.

Finding ways to put the Model T to work became such a preoccupation with handy farmers and machine shops that Ford had to invent a truck and tractor—just to meet the demand. Both were introduced in 1917, and together with the versatile Model T, led working men into the real industrial age.

In time, Models A and B, and the V8's, would carry on where those first Fords tapered off—filling the insatiable need for cheap, dependable motor power. Again, resourceful men found a thousand amazing new uses for Henry's mechanical marvels.

As a postscript to that pioneering era, pictured on the following pages are some of the familiar, and not so familiar, ways the Ford car, truck, and tractor were used to help ease the burden of work over the years.

"I think that unless we better understand the mechanical portion of life, we cannot have the time to enjoy the trees, and the birds, and the flowers, and the green fields." Henry Ford

Gandy dancers on a rail inspection with the station agent, are pictured at Calaveras, California, in 1914. Their "speeder" is a 1913 Model T Roadster stripped of top and fenders, and converted to their pleasure with a set of flanged wheels.

Minnesota woods, 1917

John McLaren, district manager of the Virginia & Rainy Lake Lumber Company, takes his boss, J.H. Gillmore, on an inspection of timber holdings in 1917. Their Model T Touring was well-suited for this purpose—having been fitted with a big searchlight and heavy flatcar axles and wheels. Once underway, the brakeless rail speeder ran smooth as a peach—but it sailed right on through sudden stops.

Lumber company officials with their 1916 Model T Touring rail "speeder"

A specially-built 1917 Model T Ford passenger stage near Sonora, California, in 1918

Sauk Center, Minnesota, 1919

In his indispensable Ford, the ag teacher could range into the countryside to review his students' farm projects. Here, an instructor stops by a young lad's home to check his dairy records.

Visiting a farm in a 1917 Model T Runabout

A 1924 Model TT Express Truck ready to deliver milk from a New Hampshire dairy in 1926

A U.S. Army driver poses with a 1918 Model T dental ambulance at a World War I bivouac.

World War I

After Henry Ford failed in his famous pacifist "Peace Ship" crusade to halt World War I in 1915, he put his entire production capacity at the disposal of the U.S. Government. Soon, thousands of Model T's were sent overseas to help the allies. One of them was the portable dental ambulance pictured above in France—the donation of a wealthy New Yorker. At the right, a doctor and a group of Red Cross nurses in New Orleans, Louisiana, rehearse the evacuation of battle casualties with a Model T ambulance.

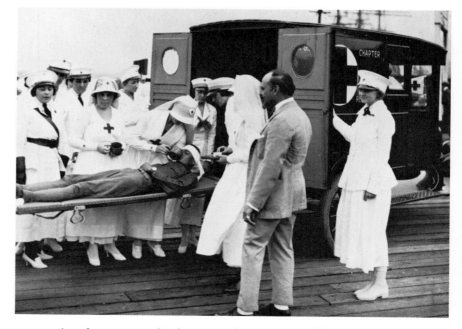

A volunteer medical unit with a 1918 Model T ambulance

One of thousands of Fords sent overseas during World War I, a 1919 Model T ambulance heads for the war zone.

A Fordson tractor pulling a disc in a Colby, Kansas, wheat field in 1918

One of the first Fordson tractors at work plowing stubble in Salina, Kansas, in 1918

Grading a Montana road in 1928 with a Fordson tractor fitted with a track-layer device

Henry's Sturdy Fordson

They were cantankerous machines that were hard to crank on a cold morning, and given to the nasty habit of rearing over backwards on the driver when pulling stumps and such. But, compared with horses and the cumbersome contraptions before 1917 when Henry Ford introduced his tractor, the Fordson did nearly as much to revolutionize rural life as the Model T. The early Fordsons were given a thousand adaptations to a thousand needs and went virtually unchanged until replaced by a new design in 1939. In the photo above, one has been converted to a powerful semicrawler, and at the right, another has been fitted with a primitive front loader to work at a rock crusher.

A Fordson loads a Model T truck with rock in Ohio in 1924.

Come haying time, the old Fordson tractor won renewed admiration from these Kentucky farmers.

Hauling a load of hay with a Model T in 1921

Boyle County, Kentucky, June, 1928

Farmers lend a hand with baling a neighbor's hay as a revved-up Fordson tractor stands off to one end of a long belt to power the stationary machine. The versatile tractor had originally plowed the field, planted it, then mowed and raked it. Now it just as handily towed the baler from haystack to haystack to finish the job. As the slapping belt spun the heavy flywheel, each man on the crew had a specific job . . . from forking hay to feed the "chinaman," to poking and tying wires, and stacking the bales.

The hired hand of a Kansas wheat farmer with a well-worked 1929 Model AA Ford truck in 1939

Junction, Texas, March, 1940

On a remote ranch in Kimble County, Texas, a Mexican contract crew shears Angora goats with power from a Ford's engine. Accustomed to working flocks on the open range, the men would drive their Model A to the isolated holding pens and jack up the left rear wheel. A special hub was then installed to run a series of belts and pulleys and enough jointed gear shafts to handle four goats at a time. During the 1930's Texas produced 80 percent of the Angora wool which was made into mohair upholstery for Ford cars.

Belt-driven shears make quick work of a goat's fleece.

Shearing goats with power from a cut-down 1928 Model A Phaeton.

All in a Day's Work

Farm chores took a heavy toll in Ford wear-and-tear but the car was a godsend to isolated folks depending on a weekly trip to town for supplies. Fresh eggs and milk were taken to the creamery and sold for cash, which in turn bought a new batch of baby chicks, a sack of feed to throw over the fender, and maybe a new dress for Ma. As for Pa, there would be tools to buy and maybe a new doodad from the mercantile store to fancy up the old Ford . . . something like a hood ornament, coontail, or a bright reflector.

Loaded front of a San Antonio 1933 Ford Pickup

Chick feed on a 1929 Model A Tudor fender at Enterprise, Alabama

Sack of feed on a 1934 Ford bumper at Brownwood, Texas

Cream cans tied to a 1930 Model A Sedan at Muskogee, Oklahoma

Those handy bumpers

Undaunted by the Model A split rear bumper, the owner of the car pictured to the left simply bolted on a bar that served as a trailer hitch and a support for the pair of cream cans he took to town weekly.

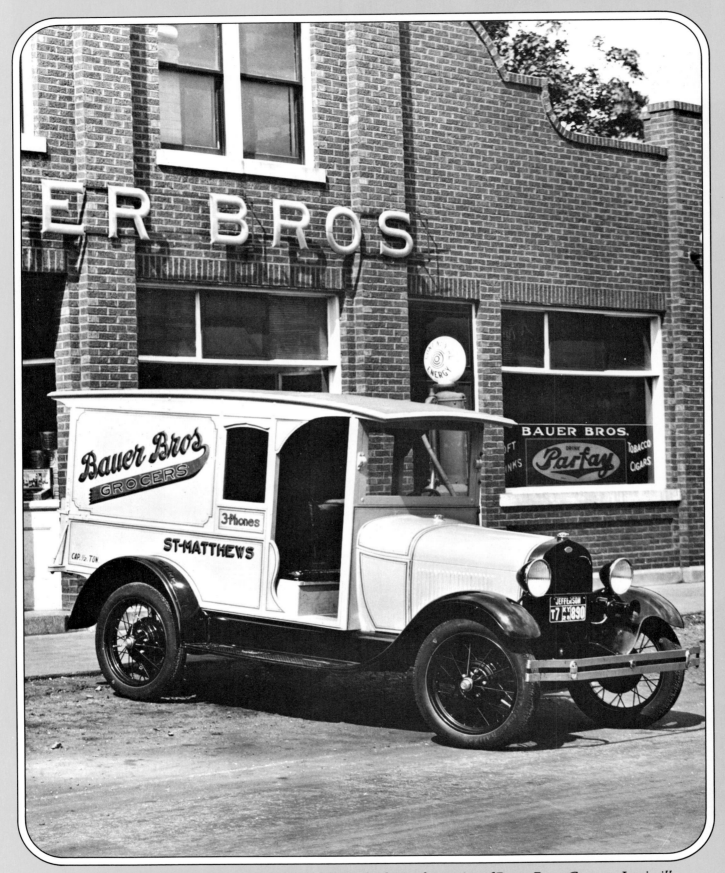

A 1928 Model A Ford, with a custom-built delivery body, in the service of Bauer Bros. Grocery, Louisville, Kentucky

A regular production 1936 Ford V8 Panel Delivery in the service of Home Laundry Company, Louisville, Kentucky

Special 1933 Ford V8 truck for an economy promotion

Louisville, Kentucky, September, 1933

As part of a company-wide campaign, Louisville area Ford dealers loaded this truck with drums of oil and sent it out on a 5,000 mile economy run. The truck, which was finished in shimmering silver, had a spotlight and carried an extra fuel tank for the fast, non-stop tour.

Pennsylvania, 1934

The hard working Ford pickup had become a familiar part of the American scene by the middle 1930's. The dandy 1934 model came with a choice of 4-cylinder or V8 engines and had a cowl and windshield that swung open to cool the interior. The one opposite has found summer duty fueling U.S. Forest Service survey planes operating from a small town landing field.

Illustration by Roy Jones

A 1934 Ford V8 pickup delivers fuel to a bi-wing camera plane as awe-struck boys look on.

Yakima, Washington, 1937

The Ford truck has been the easy favorite of American farmers. Appearing in 1937 was the light platform model that an apple grower (below) has found to be ideal for peddling baskets of fresh-picked fruit from his nearby orchard. The lady customer's sedan offers a pleasant comparison in Ford car and truck styling for that year.

A pair of farm hands in a 1928 Model A Phaeton at Person County, North Carolina, July, 1939

A young farmer selling apples at the roadside from his new 1937 Ford Stake-bed Pickup

Illustration by Roy Jones

U.S. Forest Service fire fighters with their new 1940 Ford V8 Cab-Over-Engine unit

Sierra National Forest, California, 1940

Smoke chasers at the Mariposa Ranger Station model the latest in forest fire suppression equipment. Their snub-nose Ford (a type first offered in 1938) was given extra agility over winding mountain trails with the aid of a two-speed rear axle. The unit carried backpumps and trail-building tools for the crew, a supply of water, and extra hose for a companion pumper truck.

People up front. Hogs in the back. A jammed 1941 Ford Station Wagon takes on more passengers.

The Ford dealer, and friends, from Fairfield, Ohio, visiting the big Rouge plant at Dearborn in grand style. Their 8-door 1948 Ford tour bus was custom-built by Seibert.

San Juan, Puerto Rico, September, 1941

A GI stationed at a nearby U.S. Army Base couldn't resist snapping this classic picture (left) of a Puerto Rican "Carrioca" driver breaking in his new Ford station wagon. The three-seated, wood-bodied Fords were popular taxis in the semi-tropical country. This one is carrying at least a dozen passengers, with a farmer's new brood sow lashed onto the tailgate.

Using a handy 1942 Ford Pickup to haul dairy cans at a farm in Michigan

5
Ford on the Dirt Tracks

It is little wonder that Ford and racing have been synonymous for so many years.

Henry Ford actually founded his company on his early racing exploits and became a national hero in 1904 when he set the world record for the mile in his handbuilt car. As his auto business grew over the next decade he was in and out of racing, at various times sending his ace driver Frank Kulick out to challenge the best on the dirt track and hill-climb circuits. Between 1910 and 1913 Kulick won so many races with his swift 4-cylinder Model T against the big clumsy machines that the underdog Ford became the most talked-about car in America.

Then, Ford withdrew from racing after the big-car companies conspired to set rules barring the Model T from their game. About the same time backyard amateurs, imitating the professionals, were stripping their "tin lizzies" to make speedsters—forerunners of today's hotrods. As men will do, they began racing the speedsters against each other wherever there was an oval horse track—and picking up the speed tricks by trial and error.

By 1922 the sport was well organized and the track dominance of the Model T given a big boost when equipment manufacturers—notably Arthur Chevrolet with his Frontenac—began supplying exotic overhead valve cylinder heads for the Fords. That year Noel Bullock, a hayseed 20-year-old Nebraskan, stunned racing by streaking past the favored big cars in his "home brewed" Model T to win the world's championship hill-climb up Pike's Peak. The following year at the Indianapolis "500," Ford made headlines again when L.L. Corum flashed to fifth place in his Frontenac-equipped Model T racer, behind four sophisticated Miller eight's.

Bullock went on to become a legend on the dirt tracks, racking up 74 wins with his car in six years. Other greats like Frank Lockhart, Lou Meyer, Fred Frame, Babe Stapp, Kelly Petillo, and Howdy Wilcox came out of the dust of Model T racing to make it big at the Indy "500."

Serious Model T racing waned in 1932 with the arrival of the Ford V8, but the dirt tracks continued to be just as exciting. Over the next three decades Ford would still rule the sport as speed enthusiasts discovered stock cars, midgets, and hardtops.

". . . Dirt track races are won or lost on the turns, so driving the turns fast is especially important. . . . Don't shut off—but make all turns with the engine pulling. Then you can tool the car to any part of the track you wish. . . ."

Arthur Chevrolet, builder of
the Fronty-Ford, 1926

Fords terrorized the dirt tracks. A driver sets up his Model A-powered racer for a turn at Cleveland's Brook Park track about 1938.

Auto race fans, waiting for the gates to open at an Indiana dirt track in 1926

Washington, D.C., 1922

Amateur dirt track drivers and their mechanics are pictured at the right, battling with their home-built Model T racers past the grandstands at Bennings Field in Washington. The offbeat variety of radiator and body shapes attests to the flourishing Ford speed equipment business that had developed by the early 1920's. With catalog in hand, a serious car builder could choose from bodies by such makers as Race-Way, Bub, Mercury or Ames; overhead-valve engine heads from Rajo, Roof, Frontenac, or Hal; wheels from Houk, Dayton, or Buffalo; carburetors from Zenith or Winfield; and ignition systems from Atwater-Kent, Kingston, or Bosch.

Frank Kulick, winning with his Model T at Syracuse, N.Y., in 1911

Promoting the Model T Racer

It wasn't by chance that the Model T became an early racing hit. For publicity, Henry Ford sent some hopped-up cars on a barnstorming tour of the country between 1910 and 1913. His hand-picked driver was Frank Kulick, who would take the jack rabbit-quick Fords to an astonishing string of flat track and hill-climb wins. On a single afternoon at New Orleans in 1911, Kulick won four major races in his spindly 20hp Model T, beating out big 100hp Buicks, Fiats, Nationals and the like.

Model T's were cheap and fun to race. An odd assortment slides around a turn at a Washington track in 1922.

Los Angeles, California, 1927

A dashing driver has his Ford-powered race car fueled at a downtown service station. Actually, it was a staged publicity stunt for a Shell Oil Company ad. Dual carburetors off the side of a Rajo overhead valve set-up meant this car was as fast as it looked.

Louisville, Kentucky, 1931

Pictured below, in front of his sponsor's shop, a race car driver exhibits the latest in 1931 dirt track machines. Powered by a Fronty-Ford overhead valve Model T engine, his rakish car has a jazzy paint job, knock-off wire wheels and gas cap, and shock absorbers.

Filling up for a fast afternoon at the track

A local speed burner poses with his freshly-built Ford racer in 1931.

Louisville, Kentucky, 1926

Typical of the professional-type dirt track racers built in the heydey of the Model T is this speedy underslung machine modeled by a young mechanic. Based on the Ford engine and chassis, it featured a hand-formed body, narrowed frame and radiator, Frontenac 8-valve head, Hewitt Cord tires and wire wheels. Created by entrepreneur Arthur Chevrolet, the legendary Frontenac set-up was the widely used speed equipment which enabled a Ford racer to place a fast fifth in the 1923 Indy ''500'' against the big cars.

Model T's, with their strong, wiry chassis, were ideal for racing.

A future track champion tries out a 1926 Model T racer.

Rewarding a champion Ford race car driver at Ascot in 1927

Illustration by Roy Jones

A potent Model T dirt track racer at Ascot in 1927

Illustrator Roy Jones captures some pit action in 1927 as driving ace Speed Hinkley accepts a trophy won behind the wheel of a buddy's fast bob-tail Model T racer. Mechanics and railbirds look on as cars beyond get ready for the next heat. The scene was at the popular Legion Ascot Speedway near Los Angeles.

Alhambra, California, 1927

Southern California speed king Francis Quinn has his Rajo-equipped Ford all set up to take the next race. Notice the leather straps tying the buggy springs down to stiffen the suspension. Each track was a unique challenge, and the drivers had to be more than fearless top-notch mechanics, but shrewd innovators also. Many learned their skills on the dirt, as here at Ascot, and graduated to bigger things. In 1931 Quinn qualified a Model A Ford-powered car in the Indy "500."

At the Kentucky State Fairgrounds track in 1931, daring locals flash by in a cloud of dust during the intermission free-for-all while the cars from the main event cool in the infield. As usual, well-tuned Ford racers and nimble jalopies predominate the scene.

Famed Indy "500" driver Wilbur Shaw and a stock 1934 Ford Roadster.

Detroit, Michigan, October, 1933

The sensational 1932-34 Ford roadsters were converted from street form (above) to track (right) by discarding fenders, etc. The most famous was Fred Frame's Elgin (Illinois) National Road Race winner, which is shown proudly exhibited at the 1933 Ford Exposition of Progress. The speedy car led Ford V8s to the first six places in the 203-mile race.

Fred Frame's 1933 Elgin Road Race winner.

By stripping off a few excess parts, the 1934 Ford Roadster made a natural stock car racer.

Oakland, California, 1934

When the Ford V8 made its appearance in 1932, race car drivers gave it a try out on the track. To their joy they found that the Roadster, with its removable windshield and top assembly—especially the 1933-34 models— made the fastest, most agile stock cars in racing. Here, a driver and his hefty mechanic strip their roadster of its street equipment for a contest at the Oakland Speedway in 1934.

Officials scrutinize a Ford V8 engine.

Long Beach, California, February 17, 1934

Following Elgin, the next major stock car race in the U.S. was held at Los Angeles Municipal Airport (Mines Field) in 1934. That Fords held drivers of other makes in total awe is demonstrated by the fact that of 26 cars entered in the Gilmore Gold Cup Race, all but four were Ford V8s. At the right center a Rockne and a Chrysler are worked on in a crowd of Fords the afternoon before the race. In the photo above a mechanic stands by while AAA track officials qualify his V8 engine for entry.

Inside the hangar at Mines Field where mechanics tuned up the contenders for the 1934 Gilmore Gold Cup.

A Ford V8 laps a Plymouth in the 250-mile 1934 Gilmore Gold Cup Race.

A pair of Ford V8 roadsters battle up a steep incline in the 1934 American Targo Florio road race.

Lou Meyer takes the inside to pass Swede Smith and Bill Froelich in the Gilmore classic.

Los Angeles County, California, 1934

In February, 1934, seventy-five thousand fans saw Stubby Stubblefield's Ford V8 nose out Pacific Coast champion Al Gordon to win the Gilmore Gold Cup and the $3,500 prize money. Two months later at the outlying Ascot Speedway a similar purse attracted some more big names in AAA stock car racing. This time it was the American Targo Florio Hill Road Race, styled after a famed course in Sicily. The 1½-mile circuit utilized most of the half-mile Ascot oval track, then veered off into some steep hills for the rest of the distance. Ford V8s took the top ten places in this 150-mile event, with celebrated driver Louis Meyer dueling it out with Ted Horn for the win.

Driver Johnny Seymour (coveralls) and mechanics work on one of the Miller-Tucker-Ford cars during qualifications.

Harry A. Miller (hat) with driver George Bailey and one of the 10 Ford-sponsored cars for the 1935 Indy "500." Ford also lent the pace car and a fleet of "official" cars.

Henry's Try at Indy

Model T "Fronty-Fords" first began racing at the famed Indianapolis "500" in 1921 (one placed 5th in 1923) but it wasn't until 1935 that Henry Ford sponsored an entry. Through Edsel, promoter Preston Tucker (later, Tucker car debacle), sold the reluctant auto magnate on the idea to finance 10 racers to be built by speed genius Harry A. Miller. The cars would be entered in the 1935 classic. Starting from scratch, Miller designed the cars around souped-up Ford V8 engines turned around backwards to fit a quickly-engineered cast aluminum front-wheel-drive set-up—and had them all at the brick track in just 79 days! The beautifully streamlined Miller-Tucker-Fords caused a sensation with the press but only four qualified for the race because the steering gears tended to overheat. None of the four cars finished (three went out with steering problems) and what might have been a major publicity triumph became Henry Ford's only try at Indy.

The 1935 Ford racers were the first at Indy to combine front-wheel-drive and four-wheel independent suspension.

Driver Ted Horn, and his mechanic Bo Huckman, made the best showing by lasting 145 laps before the ill-fated steering box froze. They placed 16th.

Unloading a Ford-powered midget racer from the trailer of a 1940 Ford Deluxe Station Wagon at a Midwest track in 1941.

Midgets and Hardtops

Ford continued to dominate dirt track racing through the 1940's and 1950's. When the small 60hp V8 engine came out in 1937 as an economy option to the bigger 85hp block, builders stuffed them into scaled-down Indy-type chassis and the quarter-mile "midget" racing craze was born. Then, after WWII with most of the fast soft top Ford roadsters in the hands of hotrodders, stock car racers began gutting 1937-40 (most popular) Ford coupes and modifying them for newly created "hardtop" events. This activity hastened the departure of these types from the streets as it seemed that every garage and service station was torching a Ford hardtop to sponsor. The secret to winning was a well-tuned flathead V8, a Lincoln-Zephyr transmission linked to low 4:44 or 4:11 rear axle gear ratios, the left side of the frame tied down and right side jacked up with bigger tires —and a lead-foot driver. The almost destruction derby-type hardtop races were often run on larger ovals between the midget events and both were extremely popular with spectators well into the late 1950's.

For the weekend oval racer, the Ford V8 hardtop was the biggest

154

Bob Rushing with his 1937 Ford V8 Coupe hardtop racer, between heats at the Oakland (California) Speedway in 1950.

thing since the dirt track Model T. Three 1937-40 coupes mix it up on a turn at the Oakland Speedway in 1950.

6
Ford Graffiti

For the all-American boy with real gasoline in his blood, there was never anything quite like a Ford.

Youth began its happy-go-lucky romance with the machine back in the days when cast-off Model T's were so cheap that a kid could oftentimes get one free—just for cleaning up the neighbor's yard. It was one of life's great adventure stories as thousands of wide-eyed teenagers with flat pockets and big ideas hammered and banged away on the old relics—over the family horselaugh and the half-hearted complaint that junior was spending too much time on the piece of junk.

But it was the wonderful age of shade tree innovation and out of that motley of wisecracks, skinned knuckles, rusty tin, and broken motors came a craze that swept the country from high school parking lot to college campus. It was the phenomenon of the Ford hotrod—first as the fixed-up Model T jalopy scrawled with hep graffiti and then, as Model A's, V8's and Mercurys came into the picture, the chopped, channeled, and customized cars with their souped-up engines.

All this enthusiasm for the Ford automobile among the younger set was not without its champions in Dearborn. Henry Ford fired those early passions with his straight-laced, but seductive Model T, and his sophisticated son Edsel will long be remembered for the adventurous Model A and V8 body styles. But after World War II, when they were gone and Edsel's young son Henry II took charge of the Company, came the first conscious effort to build cars with the young-at-heart in mind.

Here is a sentimental look back at some of those great cars and special moments that have made the Ford so popular through the years.

Kids were crazy about Model T's. On a cross-country lark in 1923, four young fellows pose with their graffiti-mapped jalopy at a stop in Olympia, Washington. They had started in Los Angeles and were singing for gas money to New York.

Three kids with a 1931 Model A Roadster jalopy—better known as "The Yellow Bullet"

Belle Glade, Florida, June, 1940

Two guys and a gal, in town Friday night with their hot jalopy, check out the action on Main Street. Their rag top Ford has had a lot of hard use and a brush paint job since it was a spiffy two-tone roadster with a rumble seat and fancy luggage rack. These days it's a thrill a minute with smoking tires, slammed gears, breakneck speeds, and the latest hep talk painted all over the still-willing old body.

Washington, D.C., May, 1942

Cast-off Fords have always served some-one farther down the economic scale. In the '40's, especially, kids would pick up the old relics for $30 or $40, paint on some faddish graffiti and have an instant, personalized, jalopy. At the right, some capitol city college students try to impress a proper young lady with their zany Model A.

Chapel Hill, N.C., October, 1940

Two University of North Carolina freshmen, in the photo below, clown around off campus with their decorated "bucket of bolts." These old Ford "tubs" with their throw-away tops and rugged interiors made dandy open air jalopies that could be had for a song and were often passed on as mascots from class to class.

Making time with a jazzy 1929 Model A Roadster jalopy

A 1928 Model A Phaeton—one of the most popular Ford jalopies

California boys, too young for service, pitch in to collect WWII scrap.

Some Montana kids out for a spin in the snow with their makeshift Model T jalopy

Judith Gap, Montana, March, 1942

Take four teenage boys and an old abandoned Model T chassis and you had the makings of a country-style jalopy. One kid was always a born mechanic and had the rusty engine running before they found some wheels to stick on. The others were good scroungers and came up with an old touring car windshield, some boards and a Buick seat cushion to sit on, a vacuum fuel tank system out of an old Packard, and other odds and ends to make it run. No driver's license required; no registration necessary—just kids having good clean fun. The cops looked the other way. Get together 20 cents for a gallon of gas and away you went!

San Juan Bautista, California, May, 1942

Volunteer schoolboys (left page) scrounge their neighborhood's backyard junk heaps with enthusiasm during the nation-wide WWII scrap drives. Ironically, the industrious Japanese-American youngsters would soon be interred for the duration. In their trailer, remnants of Fords bound for greater glory are seat springs, a spare wheel band cover, and a rumble deck lid.

Pasadena, California, May, 1941

Hotrodding (as pictured here) evolved directly from the Ford speedsters and jalopies of the '20's and '30's—nurtured by seat-of-the-pants speed equipment makers and the phenomenal popularity of the fast flathead Ford V8 engine. Just before World War II, Southern California was the main focus of this activity, with young men hopping up every Model T, A, or 1932-34 Ford roadster they could lay their hands on. The midnight runs over the San Gabriel mountains to the vast dry lakes in the hot Mojave was their road test—the impromptu races in the dusty alkali, their proving ground. Weight and wind-resistance was the enemy, so fenders and running boards came off and front-ends and windshields were dropped and chopped. Out of this milieu came the potent, but generally street legal, American hotrod.

Pioneering Southern California rodders (as below) in 1941.

Members of the "Gaters" roadster club—one of dozens of such hotrod clubs which sprung up in Southern California

Through the swapped parts, cars are identified left to right as: 1929, 1934, 1929, 1932, and 1934 Ford roadsters.

just before WWII—pose with their rods in Pasadena in 1941. All are Fords and more than half are 1932 roadsters.

The Legendary Dry Lakes

A string of dry lake beds in the Mojave Desert east of Los Angeles was a magnet to daring young men in quest of all-out speed. Here at Muroc in the early 1920's, and later at El Mirage and others, they brought their modified street cars to see how fast they could make them go over the hot desert floor. At first it was a loose contest of all makes, but the lighter, stronger, faster Fords began to prevail and soon the flathead V8's ruled the dusty flats. It was an exciting time to be interested in bores and strokes, manifolds and headers, cams and cranks, and a place for names like Winfield, Cragar, Riley, Meyer and Edelbrock to prove their Ford speed innovations and become hotrod legends. It was a place that would have a lasting influence on the performance of the modern American automobile.

George Ausborn's '27 T-bodied V8 roadster at El Mirage in 1947

A Stoker Club member's A-bodied V8 roadster at Muroc in 1941

Fords ruled the Mojave dry lakes. Speed enthusiasts watch some roadsters line up for a match at El Mirage in 1946.

Rolling toward the starting line, a Ford roadster gets a push start at El Mirage in 1953.

El Mirage, California, 1953

For a hot engine, some skinned knuckles and a few bucks for gas, a fellow could be a weekend hero at the dry lakes. The typical runner in the '40's and '50's was this Ford (above) built by Ray Calvi. It consisted of a stripped 1928 Model A roadster body bucket and hood, '32 radiator shell, dropped axle, ''juice'' brakes, and a stroked Mercury flathead.

High school teenagers in a 1934 Ford 3-window Coupe watch a car go by just like theirs . . . almost.

A brand new 1934 Ford Standard "5-window" Coupe at Long Beach, California

Illustration by Roy Jones

Pasadena, California, 1953

The Ford coupe made a natural street rod. Kids in the '50's loved to get their hands on real straight ones and "modify" them a bit—like chopping the top a few inches, dropping the front, hopping up the flathead V8, and adding jazzy wheels, "juice" brakes, Tijuana upholstery, and a wild paint job. In this scene a teenage couple watch a "little old lady" ghost by in a car rarely sighted—and coveted by every hotrodder in town.

The Ford Customs

Personalized Fords had been around since Model T days, but it wasn't until the mid-1930's that body customizing really took off—reaching a peak of interest in the late 1950's. How far the fad had progressed by 1941 is nicely illustrated by the photo at the top of the facing page. The 1936 Ford Coupe has a well-balanced design with a good fit of the chopped top and window openings. Other early-custom features of this car are: filled stock grille with shortened Lincoln-Zephyr grilles in the fender aprons; solid hood panels; chrome strips replacing the running boards; rear fender rock guards; Buick fender skirts; and ripple hub caps with ''flasher'' bars. Pictured right is a typical well-crafted custom in 1952. This car began as a 1938 Ford Convertible Sedan and was channelled, dechromed, and fitted with a 1940 Ford Deluxe front-end and a Carson/Hauser fixed top.

Ray Vega's 1938-40 Ford Convertible Sedan at Los Angeles in 1952

John Geraghty's customized 1940 Ford Convertible at Los Angeles in 1953

A customized 1936 Ford 5-window Coupe at Santa Monica, California, in 1941

Customized 1937 Ford Cabriolet in California about 1938

Detroit, Michigan, 1950

Ford Motor Company was well-tuned to the latest trends when it posed this promotional shot (right) at a suburban drive-in. The idea was to show American youth what great fun was awaiting the purchase of a new Ford convertible.

Burbank, California, 1953

Pictured below, some owners with cars modified by Valley Custom (a legendary Southern California shop) gather for an outing. In the foreground is Ron Dunn's trend-setting 1950 Ford Coupe. Beyond may be seen Ray Vega's 1938-40 Ford Convertible Sedan and Ralph Jilek's '40 Ford Convertible.

At the drive-in with a new 1950 Ford Convertible

Cars by Valley Custom, out for a drive near Los Angeles in 1953

Illustration by Roy Jones

An after school stop in a 1950 Mercury Convertible. Hanging out at the local drive-in was the teenage national pasttime.

Santa Rosa, California, 1954

One sure way to a girl's heart was a Merc convertible with the top down, and a cruise to the drive-in for a milk shake. The 1949-51 Mercury coupes and convertibles were very popular among youth in the 1950's and the next best thing to an all-out customizing was a couple of sacks of sand in the trunk for the right lowering effect, fender skirts, baby spotlights and wide whitewall tires. Gordon's Drive-in on Fourth Street in Santa Rosa was a classic example of the many carhop restaurants which flourished during that period.

The big Ford event of the 1940's was the introduction of the totally new 1949 models. At Louisville, Kentucky, a dealer and his staff, and curious onlookers, pose outside the crowded salesroom with a pair of the modernistic tudor sedans on show day, June 8, 1948.

173

The typical young American couple looks over a modest 1952 Ford Crestline Sunliner Convertible.

The Early Fifty's

The distant war in Korea had caused scarcities of such luxuries as heavy chrome plate and whitewall tires, but Ford's progressive styling and liberal terms stayed at the leading edge of the booming market that kicked off the 1950's. To promote the idea that every young family could afford one of their cars, Ford publicists in Dearborn posed the smiling couple above admiring a new model at Stuart Wilson Ford—just down Michigan Avenue from Company headquarters.

A pleased owner with her fashionable new 1954 Ford Crestline Sunliner Convertible

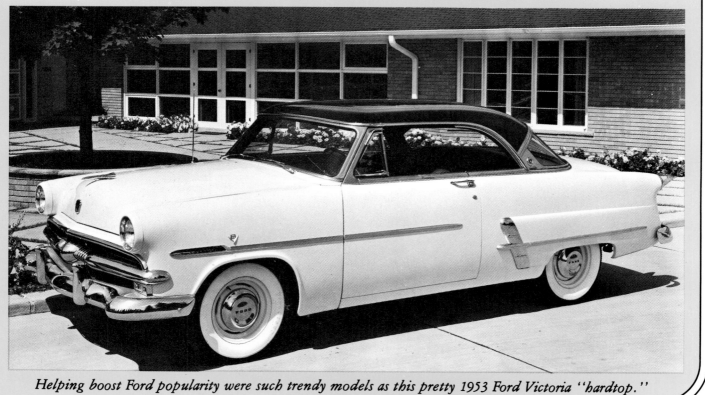

Helping boost Ford popularity were such trendy models as this pretty 1953 Ford Victoria "hardtop."

Smoothly customized 1953 Ford Victoria by Charles and Frank Gilardone of Detroit, Michigan.

Radical 1948 Continental Cabriolet creation by Detroiter Raymond P. Jones

Star attraction at the 1956 Rotunda Ford Custom Car Show was the potent "Glass Slipper."

Chopped and channeled 1932 Ford 5-window Coupe built by Ernest Weiser of Hamilton, Ohio. It had an Olds engine.

Dearborn, Michigan, February 10, 1956

At the height of the custom car craze, Ford invited amateur builders of the top ten in a contest to exhibit their creations at the Company's famous Rotunda show building. The Ford Custom Car Show ran for two weeks "as a means of encouraging young men with a talent for creative ideas in automotive styling" and was limited to Ford, Lincoln, and Mercury cars. Outstanding among the exhibits was the lavender-colored "Glass Slipper," designed and built by brothers Ed and Ray Cortopassi of Sacramento, California. Originally powered by a '48 Mercury engine, and a top eliminator on the West Coast, the pioneering rail job was considered the most beautiful dragster in America.

The dream car at the 1956 Rotunda show was this customized 1940 Mercury Convertible built by Jerry Yatch.

Dearborn, Michigan, February 10, 1956

Prized by car customizers were the Mercurys with their wider stance, larger dimensions, and more horsepower under the hood than the Ford. Two of the all-time favorite models to modify are shown on these pages at the 1956 Ford Custom Car Show held at the Rotunda. Both cars have shaved hood, deck, and body trim, filled seams, frenched headlights, twin spotlights, and nicely proportioned chopped tops. The Yatch car has a later bumper, padded Carson-type top, and 1956 Olds 98 hubcaps. The Volpe brothers' car was a real work of art, with several inches sectioned out of the lower body in a horizontal line all around, beginning at a point at the top of the front bumper. This low beauty was further altered with moulded-off parking lights, reworked grille and later bumpers, a set of ever-popular Cadillac hubcaps, push-button door handles, and a 24-coat, hand-rubbed lacquer paint job.

Stock 1940 Mercury Convertible

Twin brothers Leo and Ray Volpe exhibited this crowd-pleasing 1948 Mercury Coupe at the Rotunda in 1956.

The fancy Ford Crown Victoria, with either glass or hard top, made its debut with the 1955 line.

The American dream in 1956—a nice home in the suburbs with a new Ford Victoria parked in the drive

Class of 1955-56

The mid-1950's were classy times for the Ford romantic. Americans seemed to have more money, more leisure time, more good reasons to buy a new car, and a lot more choices than ever before. The 1953 Ford models saw the last of the sentimental old flathead-type V8 engines and by 1955 buyers were clamoring for the dazzling selection of colorful new body styles with the optional overhead valve V8 engine.

Keeping a tennis appointment in a sporty new 1955 Ford Fairlane Sunliner Convertible

Teenage idols James Dean and Natalie Wood in a scene from the epic 1956 motion picture Rebel Without A Cause. *Dean built the low-slung 1949 Mercury Coupe semi-custom for a starring role in the film.*

Los Angeles, California, 1956

On a warm night out to a drive-in theatre to see James Dean in *Giant*, all eyes in the center rows are on a flashy new Thunderbird and its alluring blonde passenger. Sensational when they first appeared with the 1955 line, the sporty early Thunderbirds (1955-57) are considered among modern day classics. Their popularity was given a further boost by the starring role of the ghost-like white 1956 model driven by Suzanne Sommers in the celebrated 1973 film, *American Graffiti*.

Illustration by Roy Jones

Tilts and Tailfins

Keeping up with the Joneses found its counterpart in the auto industry by 1957 as manufacturers tried to outdo each other with clever styling ideas. Ford's new look included a swept-wing tail treatment and a tilt hood borrowed from the Thunderbird. Tilts were really big that year as Ford introduced the industry's first retractable hardtop—that disappeared under a tilting rear deck lid. The highlight of 1958 Ford designs would be the new quad headlights.

Showroom visitors at Cort Fox Ford, in Los Angeles, study a 1957 model with the novel tilt hood.

Tail fins were the rage. Agency models pose in an idyllic setting with a new 1957 Ford Fairlane Sunliner Convertible.

A swell idea that wasn't practical. Ford brought out the Retractable Hardtop in 1957 (1958 model pictured) but dropped it at the end of 1959.

The Sleek Sixties

Heading into the 1960's, the Fords began taking on a longer, smoother, more sophisticated shape. Tail fins gradually faded away to less-flamboyant body sides as the cars held more purely to that timeless designer's adage that "form should follow function." Mid-decade found Detroit fascinated with the youth-oriented performance market and the re-shaping of the entire Ford line—including the introduction of the sensational new Mustang—to meet that demand.

1960 Ford Galaxie Sunliner Convertible

1961 Ford Galaxie Victoria Sunliner

Sportiest of the bullet-shaped 1961-63 Thunderbirds were the roadsters (1962 pictured) offered in 1962 and 1963.

1965 Ford Galaxie 500 XL Hardtop

The Mustang brought back that old Model A magic. A 1966 GT Convertible takes a pretty Homecoming Queen on review.

Mustangs Forever!

Few cars have had more all-round youth appeal than the Ford Mustang. First introduced in mid-1964 with a variety of body styles and options, they would become the biggest Ford sellers since the legendary Model A. The convertible was a natural choice to carry this newly-crowned Homecoming Queen on her victory ride around the field during the big football game.

Fords Into the Future

The romance with the Ford automobile is destined to continue. After more than a decade sidetracked with the rest of the industry wrestling with the problems of safety, emissions, and fuel economy, Ford Motor Company entered the 1980's with the promise to once again "put the fun back into driving." Stars of the 1983 offering were the sporty new Mustang Convertible and the sleek Thunderbird. The Mustang soft top was the first in the Ford line since 1973 and put the focus back on performance with a hot 5.0 litre V8 engine. In sharp contrast to the boxy shapes of the '70's, the 1983 Thunderbird's slippery lines portend even greater things to come.

The Ford Convertible is back, with the 1983 Mustang.

The new 1983 Thunderbird promises to be one of the most exciting Ford cars in years.

Picture Credits

2:National Archives, 5:Gary Perrin, Fred Usher, 8:Library of Congress, 10:National Archives, 13:Ford Archives, 14:National Archives, 15:Library of Congress, 16:Manning Bros., 17:Tacoma Public Library, 18:Tacoma Public Library, 20:Library of Congress, 22-23:University of Louisville, 24-25:Library of Congress, 26-27:Tacoma Public Library, 28:University of Louisville, 29:(top)University of Louisville (bottom)Ford Archives, 30:Tacoma Public Library, 31:Gary Perrin, 33:Ford Archives, 34:(bottom) Long Beach City Library, 37:John A. Conde Collection, 38:(top)Ford Archives (bottom)University of Louisville, 39:(top)University of Louisville (bottom)Ford Archives, 40:(top)Tacoma Public Library (bottom)Ford Archives, 41:Gary Perrin, 42:Ford Archives, 44:(top)Ford Archives (bottom) H. Armstrong Roberts, 45:Gary Perrin, 46:Tacoma Public Library, 47:University of Louisville, 48-49:Ford Archives, 50:Library of Congress, 51:Ford Archives, 52:(top)Library of Congress (bottom)Ford Archives, 53:Ford Archives, 54:Ford Photomedia, 55:Ford Archives, 58-59:Library of Congress, 60:(top)Tacoma Public Library (bottom)University of Louisville, 61:University of Louisville, 62:Fred Usher, 63:National Archives, 64-65:Academy of Motion Pictures, 66:National Archives, 67:(top)Tacoma Public Library, 68-73:Library of Congress, 74:(top)Library of Congress (bottom)University of Louisville, 75:Academy of Motion Pictures, 76-89:Library of Congress, 90:National Archives, 91-113:Library of Congress, 115:(top)National Archives (bottom)Calif. State Library, 116-122:National Archives, 123:Detroit Public Library, 124-127:Library of Congress, 128-132:University of Louisville, 133:National Archives, 134:Ford Photomedia, 135:Ford Archives, 137:Fred Usher, 138:National Archives, 139:(top)Detroit Public Library, 140:(top) Fred Usher (bottom)University of Louisville, 141:University of Louisville, 143:Fred Usher, 144-45:University of Louisville, 146:Ford Archives, 147:John A. Conde Collection, 148-151:Fred Usher, 152-154:Ford Archives, 155:Bob Rushing, 157:Tacoma Public Library, 158-161:Library of Congress, 162-163:Bill Honda, 164-165:Dean Batchelor, 167:Long Beach City Library, 168-169:Dean Batchelor, 170:(top)Ford Photomedia (bottom)Dean Batchelor, 172-173:University of Louisville, 174-175:Ford Photomedia, 176-179:Ford Archives, 180-181:Ford Photomedia, 183:Academy of Motion Pictures, 184-187:Ford Photomedia.

The Author

Lorin Sorensen has been researching and writing about Ford Motor Company history for nearly two decades.

From 1967 to 1971 he was editor of *The V8 Times,* official publication of the Early Ford V8 Club of America; from 1970 to 1974 he edited and published *Ford Life* magazine; from 1973 to 1976 he edited and published *The Restorer,* the official publication of the Model A Ford Club of America; in 1978 he authored *The Ford Road* commemorating the 75th Anniversary of Ford Motor Company. He has also written and published four volumes in the *Fordiana Series,* and the 1982 release, *The Classy Ford V8.* Lorin is often called on by various departments of Ford Motor Company to do special creative projects such as the illustrations for the annual Motorcraft calendars.